TABLE OF CONTENTS

It is with great
joy to say to you that you are a
MIRACLE
& you have Greatness in and outside of you

Dr. Renee Sunday

THE PLATFORM BUILDER

VISIONARY OF GOOD DEEDS
MAGAZINE

We are so busy that we forgot to show appreciation for the thing we have. We don't have to show gratitude only towards the significant achievements of our life.
We should be grateful for everything we have.

That is only possible when we realize that nothing is so small that we can't be thankful for it. We mostly show gratitude towards the blessings of our life on occasion or holiday seasons.

On festivals, we have our loved ones nearby, which reminds us of the benefits we have. By showing our gratitude, we feel more thankful, joyful, and proud not only on occasion but regularly.

FOCUS ON

GRATITUDE

WHY IS IT IMPORTANT?

The expression of your gratitude helps you to play your role in society and to maintain a social relationship.

Appreciation plays its role as a catalyst and initiates the happiness in your life. When we have gratitude in our attitude, we always feel blessed for what we have. When you are thankful for the things in life, it is like turning your house into a home, a meal into a feast, and a stranger into a friend.

Having a behavior of gratitude tells others you are satisfied with what you have. If you are not grateful, you are blocking the blessings that were heading towards you. The seed of gratitude nourishes your soul and give peace to your mind.

💙

BENEFITS OF GRATITUDE

When you have a grateful behavior, you experience a variety of changes in your life. Some of its benefits are:
.

Gratitude improves your mood: Being thankful for what you have improves your mood as it means you are satisfied with your life. Writing about the things you are grateful for helps motivate you for something more prominent.

Gratitude makes you healthy:
When you have an attitude of gratitude, there are fewer chances of stress and depression in your life. When you have no anxiety, it means that there are a lot of diseases you are safe from. Among other benefits, it helps you to maintain blood pressure.

A grateful person always experiences good feelings and has happier moments in life then an ungrateful person.
It helps you to improve your capability to deal with depression and other negative things in your surroundings.

Development of your personality:
Gratitude plays a constructive role in the development of your personality. It improves your vision, self-esteem, spirituality, and optimism. It makes you less materialistic and self-fish.

Gratitude rises energy levels:
Your energy levels are connected to your mental well-being. And you can strengthen it with your grateful behavior.

And you can strengthen it with your grateful
behavior. It relaxes your mind and promotes
positive emotions.

Gratitude helps you to relax:
Gratitude promotes positive
emotion that helps to relax your body and
mind. It improves your sleep, which
in turn makes you healthier.

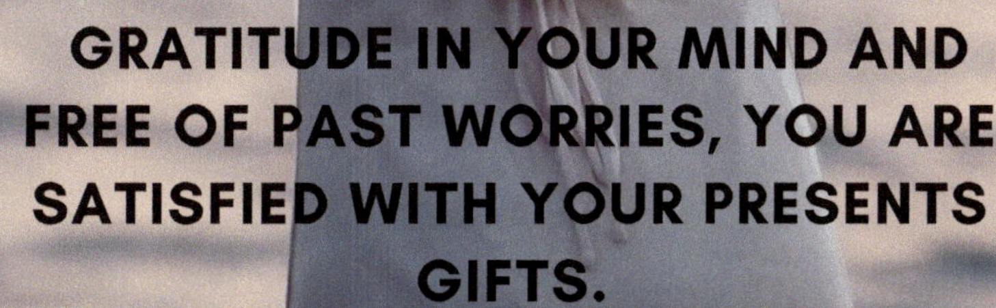

≫LOVE→≫

How to Write
Devotionals

Opening up to someone means we talk about our inner self. Our inner self is involved with different feelings and thoughts. When you want to share these emotions with another person, it means you are expressing yourself to others.

When you open yourself to others, you give them the invitation to know about your personal life. Being open is sometimes very difficult. It makes you feel anxious, vulnerable and sometimes uneasy. But it is also essential to let others know how you think, believe and think about certain situations. When you open up, the other person shares his/her experience with you.

Commonly, we hide our feelings and thoughts as we are worried that the other person will not understand our situation. When we try to prevent other people from knowing us, it means that we are not accepting ourselves. We are rejecting our chances to speak about our inner feelings and thoughts.

It is your choice to decide what you share and talk about. When you share information about your clothes, it is also a way of opening yourself to others. But if you talk about your relationship and work problems with others, it is a different thing. It means that you believe the other person will understand you and it put your conversation in a deeper level.

Choose an Honest Listener

Naturally, we cannot
share our personal information with anyone. Remember
that it is not appropriate to talk about what happens in your
life with everyone. If you don't fully trust
someone, please try not to share vulnerable information.

They can use it against you.
It would be best if you shared your personal life issues with
your close friends, not with your boss or with the person
you don't even know. Openness means you make your
inner and outer world similar. If you want to share your
personal issues to release stress, then share it with
someone who is a good listener. The person who doesn't
make fun of your emotions.

The person who will give you honest opinions according to their personal experience.

adj. reso
fem. past
Latin su
respect
or sho
for) he

There are many benefits of opening up to someone else experience. When you are trying to solve your problems, but you can't seem to figure it out, then you need a good piece of advice. Seek for the right person to get the piece of information in the right way.

By opening up to someone, experience helps you to sharpen your expertise, deepen your thoughts, and you will get the best solution for your problems. Maybe the person who you are sharing your personal story has gone through the same phase in their life and can give you thoughtful ideas.

OPEN UP AND TALK

When we are worried about something, it affects our work, relationships, and health.

In such situations, it becomes essential to open yourself to someone who understands your problem and can give you advice according to personal experience.

It helps to feel at ease and solve the challenges you are facing.

YVONIA PAYNE

What does winning or success mean to you?

Winning is success surpassing yourself and turning your dreams into reality. It is about overcoming yourself, your body, your limitations, and your fears.

When you turn yourself and turn your dreams into reality you succeed. Set goals and work toward achieving them makes a winner. Know what you want to accomplish and created a plan to be a successful.

Tirelessly, work the plan to achieve success one vision at a time. Winning and success is peace of mind, which is a direct result of self- satisfaction in knowing you made the effort to do your best to become
the best that you can become.

Success is an attitude. The true measure of success is how many times you can bounce back.

Celebrate Life Everyday
SHARE YOUR GIFTS WITH THE WORLD

How do you recover from thoughts of doubt or apprehensions related to pursuing your dream?

When you worry about what others may think or say if you do something then the self-doubt can quickly become stronger and you get stuck in inaction and in fear. When that happens remind yourself that the truth is that people do not really care that much about what you do or not do.

Believe in yourself and your ability to achieve what you desire regardless of what people may say or how they may feel. To recover from doubt I pray and ask for peace and a renewed strength to overcome negativity and naysayers.

How does Social Media Affects you?

Social Media can sometimes make us feel like we aren't successful enough, how do you manage those feelings subconsciously?

When everything is online you also sometimes get proof that you are, indeed, afraid. Try not to judge
how you are feeling but do acknowledge the emotion. Insecurity is the underlying emotion that
shapes our self-image and Fear of success is a very real but often misunderstood struggle.

We are told that technology and social media are giving us an inflated sense of self. It can cause us to feel desperate toward our partner or pull back when things get difficult.

The key thing to realize is that, in most cases, the fear is about the consequences of success, not the success itself. Self-sabotage involves behaviors or thoughts that keep you away from what you desire most in life.

It is that internal sentiment gnawing at us, saying "you can't do this." This is really your subconscious trying to protect you, prevent pain and deal with deep-seated fear. You have got to be in control of your own thoughts and emotions.

Do not let your subconscious allow you to miss out on what is for you. Do not get caught up in the numbers, likes or responses. At the end pf the day God has the final say. Keep the Faith and know what is for you will prosper with hard work and determination.

What is your PURPOSE?

Focus
Be Yourself
Dream Big

YVONIA PAYNE

Enjoy Life

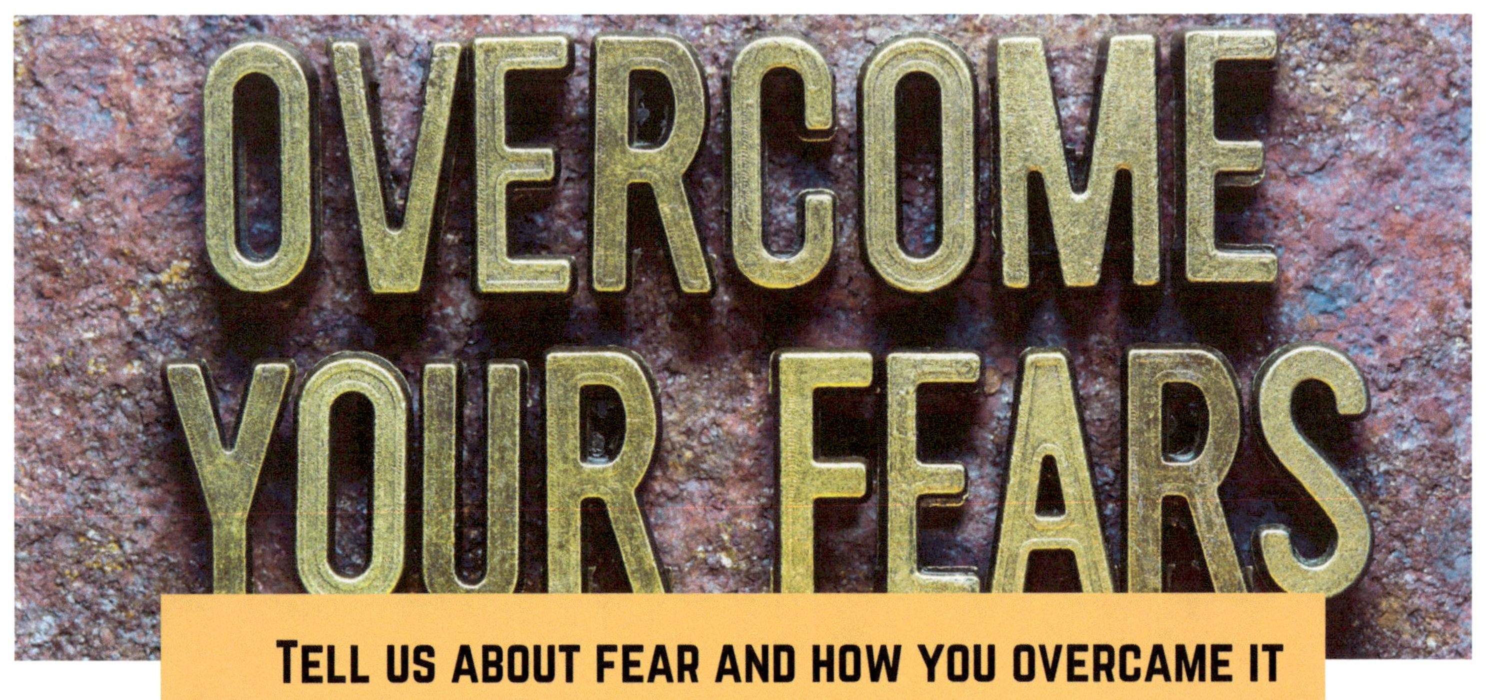

There is no more sure way to fail than to never try.
Visualize yourself now hitting an obstacle, allow yourself to
feel the fear, and then see yourself moving forward.

Think of a situation in which you are afraid of failure
and educate yourself. Next, spend a few minutes
planning how to overcome whatever obstacles may
stand in your way. How can we overcome fear?
Understand fear and embrace it

Name the fear. ..
Think long term where you are going to win
Prepare, practice, role play.

WHAT ONE PIECE OF ADVICE WOULD YOU TELL YOUR YOUNGER SELF?

Respect yourself, that is the advice I would give to
my younger self. Everything you do, all the
choices you make, your successes and your failures
are all related to how you feel about yourself.
When you love yourself and live with
confidence, your choices reflect that.

Do not worry if you feel like you have not met anyone
who's like you and you feel absolutely happy to be around.
Just be yourself and be as open as you can.
"Don't take the people you love for granted.
Tomorrow is promised to no one. "

Pruning is a horticultural and silvicultural practice involving the selective removal of certain parts of a plant, such as branches, buds, or roots.

The practice entails targeted removal of diseased, damaged, dead, non-productive, structurally unsound, or otherwise unwanted tissue from crop and landscape plants.

The same process can be done with humans. Removing diseased, non-productive, negative, jealous, unwanted individuals from your life. Respectfully, with time and patience. With every different level of my life I had to prune some things and people out of my life.

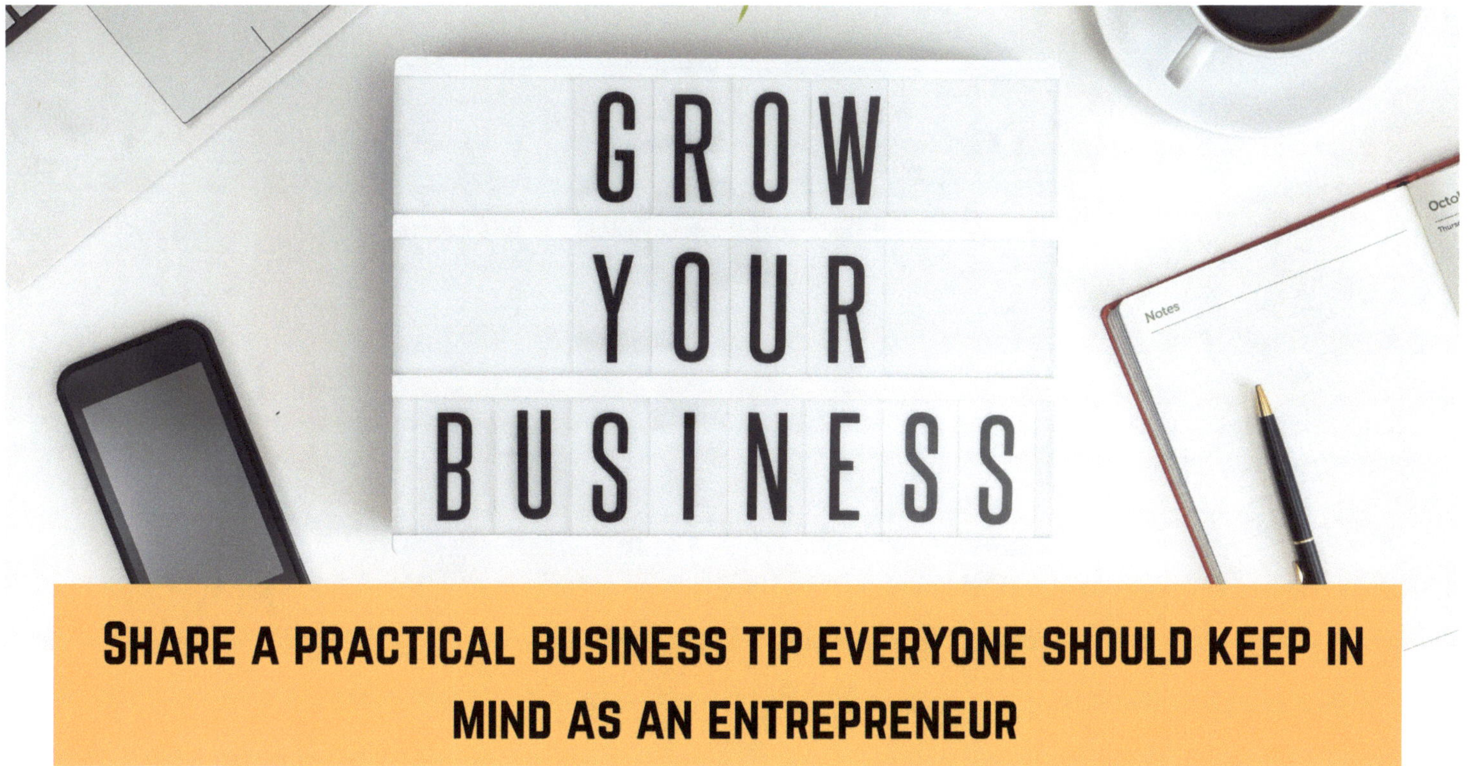

SHARE A PRACTICAL BUSINESS TIP EVERYONE SHOULD KEEP IN MIND AS AN ENTREPRENEUR

Believe in yourself and surround yourself with good people.
Someone who is successful and already
where you are trying to go.

Get a mentor have your ears turned toward those
who have your best interest in mind.

A good mentor, coach who is willing to share a few tips that
inspiring business leader should know that will help you
and your business elevate.

I own a women clothing and women and men accessories boutique. Most of the apps I use are for my boutique. I hope the app I list are helpful

Layout
Add Watermark
Photo Slideshow
Flyer maker
Boomerang
Poster Maker

Never Stop Innovating in Business or Your Love Life. Work together to set long-term goals for both family and business.

To fully love your husband and your business, you must accept your position as a wife and entrepreneur. Be willing to share all your gifts and challenges while also asserting your needs and desires.

Entrepreneurs have limited time for love, so making the most of every moment is essential. Quick tip: Organize your own wants in terms of a relationship. Some are looking for something light and fluffy and others are searching for true love.

Order at reneesunday.com

Be Grateful

She Boss

she believed
SHE COULD
SO SHE DID

Well is defined as "in a good or satisfactory manner" according to dictoniary.com. In these days and times we have to intentionally put forth effort to actually stay well. What does your does your daily schedule look like? Arise and shine, get ready for work while listening to the news.

The news report, poverty racism, homicides, sickness and disease. All the prior projections are then implanted into your mind where you unconsciously dwell on those thoughts that detract from your well-being. We have a duty to keep our mind, body and soul well. Wellness occurs when you implement a well-balanced diet, exercise, meditation and speaking positive confirmations in spite of challenging circumstances. You will always win in Christ Jesus. Be encourages, protect your health and walk in wellness every day on purpose.

3 John 1:2 English Standard Version
Beloved, I pray that in every way you may prosper and enjoy good health, as it goes well with your soul.

Benjil Lightfoot
Family Nurse Practitioner , Motivational Speaker

Order at sundayhonors.com

God did not create us to be defeated but instead, to take our place of authority. God wants you, every imperfection that you poses and every mistake you make. We rise, we may even fall and that is ok because we are human. Mistakes will be made throughout the course of this life, and as long as you are living and maturing, you will continue to make mistakes.

As we all grow and develop we will learn from our previous mistakes and teach the next generation so that they don't have to make the exact same mistakes as we did. Throughout life we will definitely experience hurt but guess what, it will not kill you.

Many times we can be our own worse enemy!! We have all done things in our lives that we probably should not have done, or may have even been in negative situations that we had no control over. Some of those things haunt many of us still to this day. It is time to stop letting your past rob you of the opportunity to have a prosperous future.

Forgive yourself, if you have already asked God to forgive you, He has done just that!! Stop continuing to beat yourself up. The only person you are only hurting you! Let it go!!! Free yourself. How do I free myself you ask, read the word of God constantly concerning healing and forgiveness!!

Every time you look in the mirror say," I forgive myself, it's over from this day forward this (say whatever is holding you back) will no longer have control over my life." Say this as often as you can out loud to yourself until you start believing that you are Free!!

Your freedom, your deliverance is in your mouth!! Proverbs 18:21 says,"Death and life are in the power of the tongue..." Speak life over yourself and you will be free!! Never expect to be perfect nor expect others to be perfect. We serve a perfect God and we should be thankful for God's grace and His mercy that is renewed daily.

We live in this world, we are not of this world. We should have so much confidence in His word that nothing we face should cause us to waiver in faith. God wants you so that He can help you in every area of your life.

You can do ALL things through Christ who strengthens you!

Marquita Humphrey

Five stress relief exercises by Cynthia Baker

Are you dealing with stress most of the day and have pressure
at work? Then it is essential to take a break or else you will be exhausted.
Our body is neither a machine nor are we robots.
As human, our body needs proper attention, and we must care for
our physical and mental health.

1.Exercise: How does exercise relief stress: Exercise plays a crucial role in
our fitness. By staying fit, you will be able to maintain both physical and
mental health. Regular activities play a vital role in dealing with your
stress by reducing anxiety and depression.

Exercise helps you to relieve stress by increasing the level of your
endorphin hormone. These are also known as the feel-good hormone of
our body.

Exercise is one of the most important things you can do to combat
stress.The benefits are strongest when you exercise regularly.
People who exercise regularly are less likely to experience anxiety .

There are a few reasons behind this: Stress hormones: Exercise lowers your body's stress hormones — such as cortisol — in the long run. It   also helps release endorphins, which are chemicals that improve your mood and act as natural painkillers.

Sleep: Exercise can also improve your sleep quality, which can be negatively affected by stress and anxiety.

Confidence: When you exercise regularly, you may feel more competent and confident in your body, which in turn promotes mental wellbeing.

Walking: Walking is probably the most effective and easiest way to relieve stress. Trust me; if you are walking in your balcony, roof, or even in the house, you are going to have a lot of its benefits.

According to studies, people who go for a walk have a lower stress level   compared to the ones who doesn't go for a walk.

2. Dancing: If you want to reduce stress in a fun way, then dancing is a good option. The good thing about it is that there are no rules to follow. You will not only feel relaxed and happy but will enjoy many health benefits.

3. Light a candle: Using essential oils or burning a scented candle may help reduce your feelings of stress and anxiety. Some scents are soothing, especially lavender and Frankincense.

4. Reduce your caffeine intake: Caffeine is a stimulant found in coffee, tea, chocolate and energy drinks. High doses can increase anxiety. People have different thresholds for how much caffeine they can tolerate.If you notice that caffeine makes you jittery or anxious, consider cutting back.

5. Write it down: One way to handle stress is to write things down. While recording what you're stressed about is one approach, another is jotting down what you're grateful for. Gratitude may help relieve stress and anxiety by focusing your thoughts on what's positive in your life.

GOOD DEEDS
Media
Network
GOOD DEEDS
MEDIA NETWORK
IS GOOD
WWW.RENEESUNDAY.COM
A few slots available to have your own
Radio Show
1 month complimentary.
36

5 MONEY AFFIRMATIONS

• I am a magnet for money. Prosperity is drawn to me.

• Money comes to me in expected and unexpected ways.

• I move from poverty thinking to abundance thinking.

• I am worthy of making more money.

• I am open and receptive to all the wealth life offers me.

• Bonus: I embrace new avenues of income.

"Prison To Power"
If God did it for me he'll do it for you!
You don't have to be in a physical
prison to be locked up.
Your mind can be locked up.
Let me show you how to go
from Prison To Power.
Who is Kent Osbourne?
Www.kentosbourne.com
38

Sam the Shark

Hi there! I am Sam!

www.ingramcontent.com/pod-product-compliance
Lightning Source LLC
Chambersburg PA
CBHW041948140726
48006CB00002BA/550